June 9, 2001

Dear Bev,

Happy Anniversary.

Love Jim.

WHAT IS THIS THING CALLED

Love?

Also by Della Reese-Lett

Angels Along the Way:
My Life with Help from Above

Coming Home

God Inside of Me

Strength is the Energy of God

THE REVEREND

Della Reese

WHAT IS THIS THING CALLED

Love?

HAMPTON ROADS
PUBLISHING COMPANY, INC.
for the evolving human spirit

For information write:

Hampton Roads Publishing Company, Inc.
1125 Stoney Ridge Road
Charlottesville, VA 22902

Or call: 804-296-2772
FAX: 804-296-5096
e-mail: hrpc@hrpub.com
www.hrpub.com

If you are unable to order this book from your local
bookseller, you may order directly from the publisher.
Call 1-800-766-8009, toll-free.

Library of Congress Catalog Card Number:00-111236

ISBN 1-57174-268-9

10 9 8 7 6 5 4 3 2 1

Printed on acid-free paper in Canada

One of the first gifts God gave to us after life and provisions was choice. For a more abundant life you need to make choices that ensure abundance. This will help you choose the great choice "love." Here is some proof about love. A life filled with love is the result of choosing to have each day filled with love. These are love seeds to plant in your mind and heart each day. And you will be able to watch love grow in your life.

Lovingly,

The Reverend Della Reese-Lett

WHAT IS THIS THING CALLED

Love?

Day One

"For God
so loved
the world
that He gave
His only
begotten Son."

John 3:16

LOVE is . . .

The ultimate expression of God.

I am Love!

Day Two

> "So . . . *I am* giving you a new commandment: Love each other just as I loved you."
>
> John 13:34

LOVE is . . . Loyalty.
You must be willing to give love anywhere, to anybody.

Because the nature of Love
Is to give,
I hold back nothing
And I give.

Day Three

> ". . . Remain in my
> love . . . so that
> you will be filled
> with joy . . ."
>
> John 15:9, 11

Jesus remained in God's love
Jesus loved God . . . God loved Jesus . . .
and, it was joy-ful-filling
When we remain in love (God),
we will be filled with joy, and
our joy will overflow.

I am loved by God
and,
I am fulfilled (joy-ful-filled), joyous.

"(So) love satisfies all of God's requirements."

Romans 13:9

Whatever the situation,
the circumstance, the appearance,
I can love *my way out of it*
because I am doing what
God wants me to do . . . giving love.

I know that each challenge
is my opportunity
to love more.

Day Five

"Love does no wrong
to anyone . . . "

Romans 13:10

I am *one with God;*
I am *one with all people;*
I am *one with all life;*
I am *one with the ONE!*

Love radiates from me!

Day Six

> "Do not nurse hatred
> in your heart. . . ."
>
> Leviticus 19:17

*LOVE is my ability to know oneness with all,
and love harmonizes me and the things
in my life, in my world, and in my affairs.*

I am learning to truly love myself from the growing awareness of how special *I am*.

Day Seven

"Love your neighbor as yourself."

Leviticus 19:18

I must love myself first in order to love my neighbor.
(If I don't love myself, I have no pattern
by which to love my neighbor.)

Because *I am* loved by God
and myself, I draw only loving
people who manifest more God.

Day Eight

"Love rejoices
in truth."

I Corinthians 13:4, 6

I address the love of the Christ in everybody.
Therefore, I let the Christ inside of me
and the Christ inside of you come together.

Love is a feeling that excites my desire for
the welfare of someone else.

Day Nine

". . . through
love serve
one another."

Galatians 5:13

And in LOVE I look
beyond the faults
and see the Christ.

I cannot love someone and abuse them.

Day Ten

"For all the law
is fulfilled in
one word."

Galatians 5:14

In giving LOVE, we receive LOVE,
for LOVE begets LOVE.

My Love is a magnet.

Day Eleven

"... the fruit of the
Spirit is ... love,
joy, peace ..."

Galatians 5:22

When we are loving,
we are joy and peace.

My love trusts and rejoices in the truth.

Day Twelve

"... the fruit of
the Spirit is ...
longsuffering...."
(Allowing Love
to take its
own course.)

Galatians 5:22

The normal attitude of love is patience.
Love is not in a hurry; love is calm.

My love sees the brighter side.

Day Thirteen

"... the fruit of
the Spirit is ...
kindness,
goodness ...
gentleness ..."

Galatians 5:22,23

*LOVE is ... an activity in kindness.
I am one with all people.*

My love is putting my best
forward in every action.

Day Fourteen

> "If ye keep my commandments, ye shall abide in my love; even as I have kept my Father's commandments, and abide in His love."
>
> *John 15:10*

Obedience is the spirit of God-love.

God is love and *I am* obedient
to the spirit of His love.

Day Fifteen

"For God has
not given us a
spirit of fear,
but of power
and of love."

II Timothy 1:7

*When God-love is established in
consciousness, it will draw to us
all that we require to make us happy.*

Divine Love expressing through me
now draws to me all that is needed
to make me happy and complete.

Day Sixteen

"He who loves . . .
abides in the light."

1 John 2:10

*God is love. God dwells in me
and I dwell in love.*

And I live in the Light.
Love is now and forevermore
my shining victory.

Day Seventeen

"... perfect love
casts out fear."

I John 4:18

*When we are established in
divine love we are not fearful.*

God as love in me is
drawing to me new courage.

Day Eighteen

". . . set your
heart
and your soul to
seek the LORD
your God.
Therefore arise
and build the
sanctuary of the
LORD God."

1 Chronicles 22:19

*Inside me I am a sanctuary of the Lord, and
through love I am a just and righteous ruler.*

I have faith that moves mountains.
I have love for my Father-Mother God,
Christ Jesus and the Holy Spirit.
Because of this I am powerful
and able to take charge of my life.

Day Nineteen

"Above all things
have fervent love
for one another."

1 Peter 4:8

*Love gives itself away. In fact,
love is not love until it is given away.*

I am in this place, or this
situation, to give love.

Day Twenty

> "... they who
> plow ... and sow,
> ... reap the same."
>
> Job 4:8

LOVE is an "as within, so without" situation.

Since I know that I reap what I sow,
I am sowing love, and *I am*
expecting my harvest to be love.

Day Twenty-One

> ". . . those
> who worship
> Him must
> worship Him
> in spirit and
> truth."
>
> *John 4:24*

God is the spirit of love within us.
Our work is done spiritually.

As my work is a spiritual work, I obey
God and allow God-love to be the
dominant power in my life.

Day Twenty-Two

"Eye has not seen,
nor ear heard,
nor have entered
into the heart of man,
the things which God
has prepared for
those who love Him."

1 Corinthians 2:9

To really live is to grow.
To grow is to change.
When we let go and let God,
we will grow through the change,
and we will be successful.
The death of the old is the birth of the new.

Because I love and trust God, I allow
the creation of new good to take place
in my life, in the midst of change.

Day Twenty-Three

"Many who are first
will be last and the
last first."

Matthew 19:30

I love first because it feels good sowing love,
knowing the harvest.

I let God-love guide, direct,
and inspire me right now.

Day Twenty-Four

"Blessed are you of the LORD, my daughter, for you have shown more kindness."

Ruth 3:10 (NKJ)

LOVE is . . . God's most beautiful daughter.

I walk in the charmed circle of God's
love, and *I am* divinely irresistible
to my highest good, right now.

Day Twenty-Five

"And we know that
all things work
together for good to
those that love God."

Romans 8:28

Love is not an emotion.
Love is a skill that we learn.

I praise Divine Love, that
there is a strong, wise, loving
way out of any dilemma.

Day Twenty-Six

"Beloved, I pray that
you may prosper in
all things and be in
health, just as your
soul prospers."

III John 1:2

*LOVE is that part of God given to us
to use, enjoy, and find peace.*

I radiate the awesome power of God-love
drawing to me the "right" people,
bringing with them the "right" situation,
and the "right" conditions.

Day Twenty-Seven

"Every man according as he purposeth in his heart (subconscious mind), so let him give."

II Corinthians 9:7

For the now and the future
I am storing and taping
Unconditional Love.

Love. Love. Love.
Thank you, God, that I give more love.

Day Twenty-Eight

". . . for God loves
a cheerful giver."

II Corinthians 9:7

The giving of love is real good *for the receiver—but marvelous for the giver.*

Because the law is, "like begets like," and love is a magnet, I know that in sowing my love, I can only reap more love.

Day Twenty-Nine

"All things were
created through Him,
and for Him."

Colossians 1:16

*As we have a thought, and we love that thought,
we can create that thought.*

As I love the thought (dream)
that I conceive, and believe
in it, I must receive it.

Day Thirty

". . . and by . . .
mighty power,
He hath given us all of
His rich and wonderful
promises. Knowing God
leads to self control . . .
leads to godliness . . .
leads to love . . . and
you will grow to have
genuine love for
everyone."

II Peter 1:4, 6, 7

True love is a divine attribute.

God is love. Love is God.
I am created in God's image-likeness.
I am created in God-love.

Day Thirty-One

> "God is love . . . he who abides in love abides in God, and God in him."
>
> I John 4:16

We rightly use the power of love when we use it as God desires us to: unconditionally.

I am the love of God in expression.

What is This Thing Called Love? is one of a planned twelve-book series, one book for each month, dedicated to providing daily reminders of God's greatest gifts.

In 1987 Della Reese-Lett was ordained as a minister by the Universal Foundation For Better Living, an organization of twenty-two churches and study groups worldwide founded by the Reverend Doctor Johnnie Colemon. Della had been teaching a class at her home in order to further the Principles that she had found so useful in her own life. What began with eight people around her dining room table has grown into Understanding Principles for Better Living Church (UP), which now has a weekly attendance of more than three hundred. Reverend Della's message of practical Christianity has been an inspiration to so many and the church is growing so rapidly that a new facility is needed and plans are underway for UP's new church home. The church maintains a web page at www.upchurch.org.

Scriptural References

Scripture taken from the New King James Version, Nashville: Thomas Nelson, Inc., 1982, and Holy Bible, New Living Translation, Wheaton, Ill.: Tyndale House Publishers, Inc., 1996.

Photo Credits

Day	Photographer
1	George Durr
2	Judalon Smyth
3	George Durr
4	Richard F. Ashley
5	Judalon Smyth
6	Tania Seymour
7	George Durr
8	Richard F. Ashley
9	George Durr
10	Stephen Black
11	Judalon Smyth
12	Stephen Black
13	Richard Ashley
14	Virginia C. Colburn
15	Richard F. Ashley
16	Virginia C. Colburn
17	Stephen Black
18	Richard F. Ashley
19	Judalon Smyth
20	Stephen Black
21	Richard F. Ashley
22	Tania Seymour
23	George Durr
24	Richard F. Ashley
25	Judalon Smyth
26	George Durr
27	George Durr
28	Richard F. Ashley
29	Richard F. Ashley
30	Richard F. Ashley
31	Richard F. Ashley

Hampton Roads Publishing Company

. . . for the evolving human spirit

Hampton Roads Publishing Company
publishes books on a variety of subjects,
including metaphysics, health, integrative medicine,
visionary fiction, and other related topics.

For a copy of our latest catalog, call toll-free
(800) 766-8009, or send your name and address to:

Hampton Roads Publishing Company, Inc.
1125 Stoney Ridge Road
Charlottesville, VA 22902

e-mail: hrpc@hrpub.com
www.hrpub.com